It's Really All Too Much...

It's Really All Too Much...

David Baird

**BARNES
&NOBLE
BOOKS**
NEW YORK

THIS EDITION PUBLISHED BY BARNES & NOBLE, INC.
BY ARRANGEMENT WITH MQ PUBLICATIONS LIMITED

2003 BARNES & NOBLE BOOKS
COPYRIGHT © MQ PUBLICATIONS LIMITED 2003
TEXT COMPILATION © DAVID BAIRD 2003

EDITOR: YVONNE DEUTCH

ISBN: 0-7607-5220-6

PRINTED IN CHINA

M 10 9 8 7 6 5 4 3 2 1

Whoever named it necking is a poor judge of anatomy.

Groucho Marx

Good company in a journey makes the way seem shorter.

Izaak Walton

Young blood must have its course, lad, And every dog his day.

Charles Kingsley

Getting talked about is one of the penalties for being pretty, while being above suspicion is about the only compensation for being homely.

Kin Hubbard

The happiest
moments of my
life have been
the few which I
have passed at
home in the
bosom of
my family.

Thomas Jefferson

15

If you would live innocently, seek solitude.

Publilius Syrus

Always be nice to people on the way up; because you'll meet the same people on the way down.

Wilson Mizner

Ability is of little account without opportunity.

Napoleon Bonaparte

Cleanliness is indeed next to godliness.

John Wesley

We have not wings we cannot soar; but, we have feet to scale and climb, by slow degrees, by more and more, the cloudy summits of our time.

Henry Wadsworth Longfellow

If the creator had a purpose in equipping us with a neck, he surely meant us to stick it out.

Arthur Koestler

Happy is the son whose faith in his mother remains unchallenged.

Louisa May Alcott

Grant me some wild expressions, Heavens, or I shall burst.

George Farquhar

The little reed, bending to the force of the wind, soon stood upright again when the storm had passed over.

Aesop

Many things difficult in design prove easy in performance.

Samuel Johnson

If you are not too long, I will wait here for you all my life.

Oscar Wilde

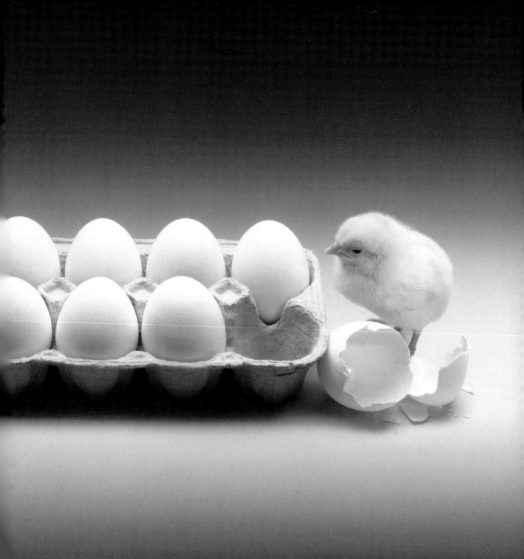

Enter on the way of training while the spirits in youth are still pliable.

Virgil

I recoil, overcome with the glory of my rosy hue and the knowledge that I, a mere cock, have made the sun rise.

Edmond Rostand

I have never been lost, but I will admit to being confused for several weeks.

Daniel Boone

Education is hanging around until you've caught on.

Robert Frost

The journey of a thousand miles must begin with a single step.

Chinese Proverb

Stands the Church clock at ten to three? And is there honey still for tea?

Rupert Brooke

The fact is that my wife if she had common sense would have more power over me than any other whatsoever, for my heart always alights upon the nearest perch.

Lord Byron

To bring up a child in the way he should go—travel that way yourself.

Josh Billings

Don't be afraid to go out on a limb. That's where the fruit is.

Source Unknown

A flatterer is one who says things to your face that he wouldn't say behind your back.

Armenian Proverb

Chase after the truth like all hell and you'll free yourself, even though you never touch its coat tails.

Clarence Darrow

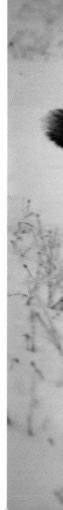

Creatures whose mainspring
is curiosity enjoy the accumulating of
facts far more than the pausing
at times to reflect on those facts.

Clarence Day

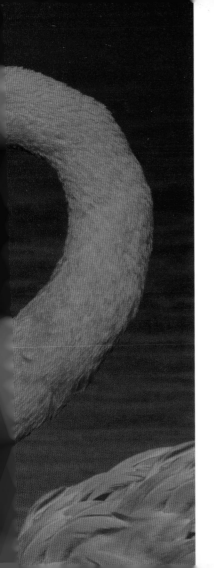

Love is not just looking at each other, it's looking in the same direction.

Antoine de Saint-Exupery

Appearances are deceptive.

Aesop

If A equals success, then the formula is A equals X plus Y and Z, with X being work, Y play, and Z keeping your mouth shut.

Albert Einstein

Get your facts first, and then you can distort them as much as you please.

Mark Twain

I am the greatest. Not
only do I knock 'em out,
I pick the round!

Muhammad Ali

In love, there is always one who kisses and one who offers the cheek.

French Proverb

In so far as God has partly revealed to us an angelic world, he has partly told us what an angel means. But God has never told us what a turkey means. And if you go and stare at a live turkey for an hour or two, you will find by the end of it that the enigma has rather increased than diminished.

Gilbert K. Chesterton

When the eyes say one thing, and the tongue another, a practiced man relies on the language of the first.

Ralph Waldo Emerson

Friendship is a sheltering tree.

Samuel Taylor Coleridge

My downfall raises me to infinite heights.

Napoleon Bonaparte

Hugs can do great amounts of good—especially for children.

Diana, Princess of Wales

He who considers too much will perform little.

Johann Friedrich von Schiller

I shall stay the way I am because I do not give a damn.

Dorothy Parker

It is better to keep your mouth closed and let people think you are a fool than to open it and remove all doubt.

Mark Twain

There is no sense in crying over spilt milk. Why bewail what is done and cannot be recalled?

Sophocles

Love is the river of life in the world.

Henry Ward Beecher

It's the height of folly to want to be the only wise one.

François de La Rochefoucauld

Photo Credits

ILLUSTRATIONS BY JANET BOLTON